THE MORNING NEWS

Carol Gray, Editor
Jenison Public Schools, Jenison, Michigan

Domestic and International Subscription Form

THE MORNING NEWS is a quarterly newsletter that informally shares practical information among parents and professionals working on behalf of children and adults with autism and related disorders. Articles address a wide variety of concerns, and share ideas which update and expand the use of social stories and related techniques and materials.

THE MORNING NEWS is available directly from Jenison Public Schools. To subscribe, complete this form and return it to us with your check, money order or purchase order to the address below.

THE MORNING NEWS makes a wonderful gift for professionals and family: If this is a gift, a gift announcement will be sent. Check the gift box in the subscription form below and indicate how the card should be signed in the space provided in the square below.

Subscription rates for one year : U.S. Subscriptions = $18.00 U.S.
Canada and Mexico= $20.00 U.S.   All other countries=$22.00 U.S.

Please print or type

Name_____Phone (optional)_____

Complete Address_____

_____

Zip Code (if applicable)_____Country_____

Please check the appropriate space: ___**New**   ___**Renewal**   ___**Gift - please**
sign gift card as follows:_____

_____

Send completed form along with payment to:

THE MORNING NEWS
Carol Gray, Editor
Jenison High School
2140 Bauer Road
Jenison, Michigan   49428

Phone: 616-457-8955
FAX: 616-457-8442

Thank You!

The New Social Story Book

The stories in this book

were carefully written for children and adults with autism

by

students in Mrs. Johnson's Psychology and Sociology classes

at Jenison High School in Jenison, Michigan.

Edited by:

Stacy Arnold
Damon Burg
Carol Gray
Kelly Goward
Sarah Hayes
Luke Jenison
Carie Jonker
Sue Jonker
Karen Lind
Joe Smiegel
Steve Wesorik
Chad Zuber
Mrs. Johnson's 5th and 6th hour Psychology classes

Cover Design, "Searching", by Janet Williams

All marketing and publishing rights
guaranteed to and reserved by

FUTURE HORIZONS INC.

Future Horizons, Inc.
720 N. Fielder Road • Arlington, TX 76012

800-489-0727 • 817-277-0727
817-277-2270 fax

www.onramp.net/autism - Website
edfuture@onramp.net - email

ISBN 1-885477-20-1

This book is dedicated to individuals with autism and those

who work alongside them to improve mutual understanding.

"The more I learn, the more I can do."

-Tyler Steketee
Social Story # 57

Preface

-Carol Gray

Social stories provide individuals with autism with accurate information regarding situations they encounter. For some students with autism, this type of written information appears to have a positive impact on their responses to social situations. Social stories have also been used successfully to teach academic skills.

This approach began early in 1991. I was observing a child with autism who was confused and disoriented by a game his class was learning in gym. I wrote a story describing the rules to the game, and the responses of other children to the game. The child read the story once each day for the following week. Upon return to gym class the following week, the child understood the rules, played the game, and enjoyed the activity. The results were so positive and immediate that stories were written for several other situations which were giving this child difficulty. These stories had the same positive impact. Because most of the stories focused on highly social situations, or situations with social implications, we referred to them as "social stories."

Joy Garand, a teacher of special needs children in Cincinnati, Ohio, learned of this approach during my presentation at the annual conference in Indianapolis that summer, and helped to expand the approach through her extensive use of social stories the following year. She had positive results, and wrote to me to share her experiences. Her stories were especially helpful in efforts to include her students in general education classes. Joy's creativity, insights, experiences and enthusiasm played a critical role in expanding the use of social stories.

By early 1992, to make the approach useful and effective for others, I began to identify guidelines for writing social stories. Joy Garand, Susan McDowell, a parent from Indianapolis, and Pat Wilson, a parent from Gary, Indiana provided early feedback from their experiences with social stories. Their ideas assisted in developing the guidelines for writing social stories. These guidelines are now continually revised and updated based on the feedback of many parents and professionals who have helped us expand our experience base.

Two major obstacles were often cited by those writing social stories. First, people were hesitant to write that first story for fear of "doing something wrong." Second, the stories were time consuming to write. Though many acknowledged the positive results, with so many possible topics the approach was often overwhelming, cumbersome and inefficient - especially for those attempting to use social stories on a wide scale.

In answer to those barriers, 250 Psychology and Sociology students at Jenison High School were trained to write social stories. The training provided them with a basic understanding of social cognition in autism, and a format and guidelines to follow when writing for individuals with autism. Each student wrote a social story, selecting a topic from ideas submitted by parents and professionals from across the country. Their collective effort produced 300 stories on a variety of topics, of which 208 were selected for the first Social Story Book. The goal was to demonstrate that "almost anyone" could write a social story with a little training, and to produce The Social Story Book 1994, to make the social story approach more efficient.

Through Social Stories, the authors are sharing what they know about the world around them with individuals with autism. It is the sincere hope of each of the Psychology and Sociology students, their teacher, Sandy Johnson, my assistants, Karen Lind and Sue Jonker, the Editors, and myself that the stories bring you much success.

We welcome your comments, your shared experiences with this approach, and your ideas which may help to further develop and improve social stories.

Acknowledgements

This book was made possible by the collective effort of many people. We wish to recognize the investment of time and creativity by the following individuals:

Janet Williams

Our cover is a copy of a pen sketching titled, "Searching," by Janet Williams, a 1994 Jenison High School Graduate. Since it is our hope social stories will provide an accurate and more easily understood look at the world and we are always searching for new ideas, we asked Janet if we could use her work on our cover. Our sincere appreciation to Janet for her exceptional contribution to this book.

Sandy Johnson

Sandy Johnson teaches Psychology and Sociology at Jenison High School. For several years, she has worked with special education staff to expand programming for students with autism. Her cooperation, enthusiasm, and investment of time were invaluable in the development of this book.

Psychology and Sociology Students

Over 250 students contributed stories for possible inclusion in this book. Unfortunately, several factors limited the number of stories we could print. The stories were terrific, and students were hopeful their stories would be a part of the book. Our thanks to the Sociology and Psychology students at Jenison High School, 1993-94, for the quality and sincerity they brought to their assignment.

The Editing Committee

Several students volunteered their time to assist in editing and typing the 100 stories in The Social Stories Book 1994. Their talent and determination literally made the final manuscript for this book possible. A very special thanks to the following members of the Editing Committee: Stacy Arnold, Damon Burg, Carol Gary, Kelly Goward, Sarah Hayes, Luke Jenison, Carie Jonker, Sue Jonker, Karen Lind, Joe Smiegel, Steve Wesorik, and Chad Zuber.

Jenison Public Schools

Our thanks to the administration and staff of Jenison Public Schools. Their acceptance, concern and support has created an environment where projects like this book can be successfully undertaken and completed. Specifically, our thanks to: Vicki Bliss and Tim Staal, who patiently shared their expertise with computers; Martha Sweedyk, for her advice and assistance; and the administration of Jenison Public Schools for their support of our efforts to share information with parents and professionals from the United States and abroad.

How to Use this Book

This book is organized into thirteen chapters. Each chapter contains several stories. A quick review of the Table of Contents will give you a general idea of how this book is organized.

You will notice page numbers are not listed in the Table of Contents, and that page numbers are not labeled sequentially throughout the book. To locate a given story, refer to the story number listed to the left of the story title in the Table of Contents. This number appears in large print in the upper right hand corner of the first page of the story. Therefore, to locate the story in the book, refer to the numbers in the upper right hand corner at the beginning of each story. Stories are numbered sequentially throughout the book.

Page numbers are listed sequentially within each story. These numbers are listed in the center of the bottom of the page. The story number is listed first, followed by the number of the page within the story. For example, the first page of story #87 is indicated as 87-1. The only exception to this are stories which contain only one page, in which case numbers are not listed at the bottom of the page. A page number at the bottom of the page indicates there is more than one page to the story.

Most stories will serve as an outline from which you can develop a final story which fits the needs of an individual student or situation. You may need to include additional details. With many of the stories, adding possible variations of a given situation may be helpful. You may wish to eliminate aspects of a story which do not apply. Some stories focus on the same topic, and may be combined and edited to draw on ideas from different authors.

Stories may be presented to a student using any one of a number of formats. The story may be placed in protective clear plastic sheets in a narrow three ring binder (business supply stores have 1" three ring binders, some with plastic insert covers, which are perfect for this). Stories may also be cut apart. The spacing between concepts in each story make this easy to do. Each concept may be mounted on a separate sheet of black construction paper. The black paper focuses attention on the printed material.

Should you wish to write your own social stories, Chapter 13, "The

Social Story Kit" covers the guidelines which will be helpful in creating your stories. Like many of the stories in this book, stories may describe literally any situation. Social stories may also address a specific social skill, for example, taking turns, handling a mistake, or speaking with the correct volume. In addition, social stories may teach an academic skill. The possibilities are endless.

Implementation of social stories often follows the child's lead, though there are a few basic strategies which may help you get started. When introducing a story, sit to the side and slightly behind the child. Explain that you have a story about_____. As you read through the story, you may want to check for comprehension. With children just learning to read, you may draw your finger along under the words as you or the child read the story aloud. Placing the story on a cassette tape, with a bell to signal the child to turn the pages may be very helpful.

Establish a review schedule for the story, with a story reviewed no more than once a day. Stories may be more effective if reviewed just prior to encountering the situation the story describes. Children often take the lead with stories, for example, indicating they "don't have to read it now." In these cases, allowing the child to review the story when he/she wants may work well, as long as the child understands you may ask that the story be reviewed if you feel it's necessary.

Stories may be faded from use using a variety of techniques. You may decrease the frequency with which the story is reviewed. A story may be faded by rewriting it, eliminating the directive sentences and leaving the descriptive and perspective sentences (see Chapter 13.) Once a child has mastered a new skill in a given situation, the story may be rewritten to generalize the new skill to additional settings.

The suggestions in this section, "How to Use this Book" are intended to define a "starting point" for using this approach. You will probably find you will write and implement each story a little differently for each individual and situation. With experience, these individual considerations will happen almost automatically.

In addition, once familiar with social stories, you may find ways to expand the approach within your program or home situation. As people already using the social stories approach have demonstrated, the ideas and applications are endless once you've mastered the basics.

"When it is time to eat spaghetti,

I put my fork in the spaghetti and slowly twirl it around.

I am careful to only put a mouthful of spaghetti on my fork,

so it will fit in my mouth."

-Erin Klooster
Social Story #34

Table of Contents

Chapter 3 : Personal Care Cont.

Chapter 4: Cooking and Mealtime Routines

Chapter 5: Helping Around the House

Chapter 6: Outdoor Games/Activities

Chapter 7: All About School

Chapter 7: All About School Cont.

Chapter 8: Getting Around

Chapter 9: Community Helpers

Chapter 10: Restaurants and Shopping

Chapter 1

Social Skills

Chewing Gum

-Danyel Orlik

Sometimes I chew gum.

I only chew one piece at a time.

I take it out of the wrapper and put it in my mouth.

I chew my gum with my mouth closed.

I leave my gum in my mouth while I am chewing it.

When my gum has no more flavor, I take it out of my mouth and put it in the wastebasket. Sometimes, before I put my gum in the waste basket I put it in a tiny piece of paper or tissue.

Giving a Gift

-Ed Staats

A gift is something you give someone.

People give other people gifts.

Some gifts are big.

Some gifts are small.

When I give someone a gift I might say, "Here's a gift for you."

It is polite to say, "Here's a gift for you."

People say, "Here's a gift for you," because it is correct.

Sometimes people give me a gift.

When people give me a gift, I will try to say, "Thank you."

Saying, "Thank you," is polite.

People like to hear, "Thank you," after they give someone a gift.

Happiness is Feeling Good

-Dave Poortvliet

Usually, when people are happy, they smile. Smiling makes people feel good. When I smile, people know I am happy.

People are not always happy. Sometimes, people are sad, upset, or frightened.

Things that I like make me happy.

Being around people I like makes me happy.

Helping Others

-Jessica DeVries

Sometimes people need help.

Sometimes people need help opening a door when their hands are full.

Sometimes people need help in other ways.

People like to be helped.

Sometimes people do not need or want help.

If I see someone who I think needs to be helped, I can ask them, "Do you need help?"

If they say "No," I will say "Okay" and I will continue whatever I was doing.

If they say "Yes," I will ask them, "What would you like me to do?" I will try to do what they ask me to do.

If I cannot do what they tell me, I will try to find someone who can.

How to Give a Hug

-Anthony Kim

I spread my arms apart.

I wrap my arms around someone.

I gently squeeze that person.

That is how I give a hug.

How to Greet Someone

-Jill Kelly

When I see someone I know, usually I will smile and say "Hello."

Sometimes I will shake their hand. Sometimes, when I am visiting a relative or a close friend, I will give them a small hug or a little pat on the back or the shoulder.

Sometimes, if I am just passing someone I know in the hall, I can smile, wave, or just nod my head. Most people like it when I smile at them. Smiling can make people feel good.

How To Make Someone Happy

-Jenny Wendt

I can make someone happy by smiling at them. It makes me happy when someone smiles at me.

I can make someone happy by hugging them.

When I say "Hi" to someone, it makes them happy.

How to Use the Telephone

-Andy Dinger

Many people like to talk on the telephone.

Sometimes grandpa or grandma will call me and we talk on the telephone.

Sometimes other people call me on the telephone.

When people call, I pick up the telephone and say "Hello."

After they say, "Hello," people ask for who they want to talk to. I ask them to please wait. Then I go and get the person who they asked to talk to.

Sometimes I will not know the person calling on the telephone. Then I will ask who is calling.

Sometimes people call and they have the wrong house. This means they have called the wrong number. I can tell them, "I am sorry. You have called the wrong number." Then I can hang up the phone.

Sometimes I want to call someone. I pick up the phone and dial their phone number.

When they pick up the phone I can say, "Hello."

I can talk to my friend on the phone.

Playing Fairly

-Andy Hoffman

It is a good idea to play fairly with my friends.

Sometimes my friend may win the game we are playing.

I will try to stay calm if my friend wins a game.

If my friend wins a game, I will ask them to play again.

It is good to play fairly at games.

Receiving a Treat In School

-Janet Williams

Sometimes someone will give me a treat.

It might be something to eat for a special occasion or just for fun.

I must make sure that I only take as many treats as the person who brought the treat offers me.

The person who brought the treat has to make sure that there are enough treats for everyone.

I will try to remember to say "Thank You," to the person who gave me the treat.

Sharing

-Mark Sheren

I can share with people. Sometimes they will share with me.

Sharing is a good thing.

Sometimes if I share with someone, they will be my friend.

Sharing with others makes them feel welcome.

Sharing with others makes me feel good.

Sharing Toys

-Melissa Keur

I like to play with toys. When I play with toys, I have fun.

Other children like toys, too.

It may be fun to play with toys with other children.

I can share toys.

Sharing might be fun. When I play, I will try to share and have fun.

Smiling

-Amy Wienczkowski

People like others who smile.

Smiling is good because it shows I am happy.

I will try to smile often.

Sometimes if I do not smile, people may think I am sad.

I may recieve compliments if I smile.

Smiling makes others feel good.

14

What I Do to Say "Hello" Without Saying a Word

-Betsy VanDam

When I meet new people, they sometimes hold out their hand. People do this as a way to say, "Hello."

I can put my right hand toward theirs and tightly squeeze their hand. I will try to make eye contact with the person and smile. Sometimes they will smile back. I let go of their hand.

I can learn to feel comfortable with this new way to say "Hello."

15

When do I say, "Thank You?"

-Julie Thomas

I will try to say, "Thank you," when someone does something to make me feel good.

I will try to say, "Thank you," when someone helps me.

I will try to say, "Thank you," when someone shares something with me.

Saying, "Thank you," may make me feel good and it also makes other people feel good.

Saying, "Thank you," is a nice thing. Other people will know I am a nice person.

When do I say, "Excuse Me?"

-Leann Moore

I say, "Excuse me," when there is a person or group of people in my way.

I am very nice to the person or group of people when I say, "Please excuse me."

I like it when people are nice to me, so I try to be nice to them.

Looking While Listening

-Brian Rowden

When someone is talking to me, I try to listen. This is a very nice thing to do.

If I look at the ceiling and other things in the room, the other person may not know I am listening.

Sometimes I try to look at a part of their face. I try to do this so the other person knows that I am listening to them. The person I am talking to will like this a lot.

Chapter 2

People and Pets

Can I hold the baby?

-Jessica DeVries

Many people like babies. Babies need to be handled with care.

If I would like to hold a baby, I will ask permission from an adult.

I will sit down while holding the baby.

I will sit quietly and move slowly.

When I am done holding the baby, I will tell an adult.

I can move when the adult has the baby in their arms.

Sometimes I will thank the adult for letting me hold the baby.

I Have a Cat

-Chad Zuber

I have a cat.

I like my cat.

Usually my cat likes it when I pet her. My cat purrs when she is happy.   When I pet my cat, it usually makes me happy, too.

I like to make my cat happy. I like my cat.

Playing with My Dog

-Becky Cunningham

I have a dog. He's big and furry and likes to play.

Sometimes I play with him. I throw a ball and he runs and brings it back.

When he's tired of playing, I might sit down with him and pet him. His fur is soft. He likes it when I pet him. It makes him feel good. I can tell because he wags his tail.

My dog can be one of my best friends.

Chapter 3

Personal Care

21

Nightmares

-Scott DeJonge

Sometimes nightmares happen when I am sleeping.

Nightmares are the same as a dream but more scary.

Nightmares do not really happen. They are in your mind.

It is all right if I am scared. I just tell myself it is all in my mind, it is only a dream.

When I wake up, I will see that I am all right.

Using the Shower

-Brandi Irvine

Using the shower can be easy and fun.

The first thing I do is go into the bathroom and close the door.

Next I take off my clothes.

I will stay dirty if I leave my clothes on when I use the shower.

After that, I turn the water on and make the water temperature comfortable. I like a comfortable temperature so I have a happy shower.

Next, I make sure the water is coming from the shower head.

When I use the shower, I stand up.

I get in the shower and get wet.

After that, I wash my hair by taking a little shampoo out of the container and rubbing it through my hair.

I like clean hair because it is nice to see and touch.

I rinse my hair off by letting the water run through my hair.

After washing my hair, I wash my body by using the soap and rubbing the soap all over my body.

Then I rinse my body off in the water.

I might like to clean my body. It makes me smell nice.

Usually when I am done, I turn off the water and then step out of the shower.

After I step out, I usually dry myself off by rubbing the towel all over my body.

I dry off so my clothes will not stick to me.

After drying off, I can put my clean clothes on. Then I am all done using the shower.

Shower

- Tom Dolce

I like to stay clean. People like it when I smell good.

Showers can be fun and refreshing.

I like to turn the water on and listen. It sounds like a slow, calm waterfall.

Then I get in and let the water fall on me.

I may like the warm water and the smell of soap on my skin.

After I clean myself with soap and use shampoo on my hair, I rinse myself off.

I dry myself off.

The shower makes me feel clean and great.

Usually I take showers everyday, they are so much fun.

How to Shave

-Patrick Elkins

Some people need to shave.

Some people do not need to shave.

When I shave, I put shaving cream on my face.

I only put shaving cream on the part of my face that I need to shave.

I am very careful with razors because they are sharp.

I take my razor and carefully shave my face.

When I am done shaving I wash off my razor and put it away.

Washing My Hands

-Carie Jonker

Sometimes, my hands get dirty. I wash my hands when they are dirty.

I go to the sink.

I turn the water on.

I get my hands wet with water.

I put soap on my hands.

I rub my hands together.

I rinse my hands under the water.

I turn off the water.

I dry my hands on a towel.

Why do I wash my hands?

-Carie Jonker

Sometimes my hands get dirty.

I should wash my hands when they are dirty.
Sometimes my hands need washing at other times.

Sometimes I cover my mouth when I sneeze. My hands get germs on them when I sneeze.

Sometimes hands get germs on them when I go to the bathroom.

I should wash my hands when they have germs on them.

I wash my hands before I eat.

My parents are happy when I wash my hands.

Why do I wear clothes?

-Kristen Diekevers

When I wake up, I take off my pajamas. I put my clothes on.

When it is cold, my clothes keep me warm.

In the summer, my clothes protect me from sunburn. I have different clothes for different seasons.

In the winter, I wear coats, gloves, scarfs and boots, because it is very cold.

In the summer, I wear t-shirts, shorts, and sandals.

When it is rainy outside, I wear a rain coat and I use an umbrella. When I go swimming, I wear my bathing suit.

Clothes help me in a lot of ways.

Wearing My Shoes

-Jamie Kinder

I usually wear my shoes when I go outside.

Wearing shoes helps keep my feet clean and protect them.

Sometimes I put one pair of socks on my feet before putting on my shoes.

I put a shoe on each foot.

It can be fun wearing shoes.

Usually mom or dad will tell me if I don't have to wear shoes.

My New Shirt

-Trapper Lukaart

I am wearing an old, worn out shirt.

Sometimes I need to buy a new one.

First I will think about what kind of new shirt I need. I might need a T-shirt, a sweat shirt, or a button down shirt.

Sometimes I go with my mom or dad to the store to buy a new shirt.

Sometimes it will take a long time to find the right shirt for me.

I look for shirts that are the colors I like.

When I find a shirt I like, I might have to try it on to see if it is the right size.

Sometimes when the shirt is the right size and color, I can give it to my mom or dad so that they can buy the shirt for me.

When I Am Sick

-Nikki Wolters

Sometimes I am sick.

Sometimes being sick makes me cough.

When I cough, tiny germs come out of my mouth.

Germs can make other people sick, too.

People do not want to be sick.

So I will cover my mouth with my hand each time I cough.

Thermometers

-Dave Sterken

Sometimes I use thermometers.

When I am sick, my mother needs to check my temperature.

I carefully hold the thermometer in my mouth, under my tongue, until my mother takes it out.

She looks at the thermometer so that she can tell how hot I am.

Usually if I am too hot, I am sick.

Chapter 4

Cooking and Mealtime

How to Make Brownies

-Megan Davis

Usually before I make brownies I ask my mom or dad if it is ok.

First thing I do when I make brownies is wash my hands.

I need a brownie mix, oil, eggs, and water to make brownies.

I need a big bowl to mix brownies in.

I read the mix box, and it will tell me how much of each thing to put in the bowl.

When I make brownies I will try not to spill. If I spill, I can get my mom or dad to help me clean up the spill.

Once the brownie mix is all mixed, I have to put the brownie batter in a greased pan.

Next the brownie batter goes in the oven. My mom or dad can help me put it into the oven.

I will always try to be careful when I am around the oven so I do not burn myself.

I read the brownie mix to find out the right time and temperature to bake the brownies. Sometimes the brownies go in the oven for about 25 minutes at about 350 degrees.

I set the timer so that I will remember to ask mom or dad to take the brownies out before they burn.

When the brownies are done, we take them out of the oven with a cooking mitt. Mom or dad wears a cooking mitt so they will not burn their fingers.

I have to turn off the oven.

I have to let the brownies cool for about 15 minutes.

I put my dirty dishes in the sink so that I can wash them.

After the brownies are cooled, sometimes I may eat one.

Sometimes I like to eat brownies and drink milk.

Eating at the Table

-Dan DeHommel

I sit at the table when it is time for me to eat.

Usually I eat when I am hungry.

I sit at the table while I am eating.

Mom likes it when I eat at the table.

How do I eat spaghetti?

-Erin Klooster

Sometimes my mom or dad make spaghetti for dinner.

I like to put tomato sauce on my spaghetti. Some people like   spaghetti plain. People eat spaghetti in different ways.

When it is time to eat spaghetti, I put my fork in the spaghetti and slowly twirl it around.

I am careful to only put a mouthful of spaghetti on my fork, so it will fit in my mouth.

If I spill any spaghetti on my face, I will try to wipe it off with my napkin.

I love to eat spaghetti.

How to Act at the Dinner Table

-Jenny Friesma

Dinner is usually the last meal of the day. It is often the largest one, too.

I eat dinner with my family most of the time. We usually eat at the dining table. We eat at the table because it is easier to talk to each other.

When I eat dinner, I only eat off of my own plate. If I want more food, I ask for it. Most people get upset if I take food off of their plate. They usually like to have their own food, like me.

When I eat my dinner, I use silverware when it is needed. I try not to spill my food on the floor, table, or other people.

How do I set the table for a meal?

-Danielle Gentit

If there are things on the table, I need to take them off and put them in a better place so they will not get dirty.

If I wash the table with a damp rag, I get the dirt and dust off so it does not get on the food I will eat.

When I set the table for a meal, I usually need to get plates, cups, forks, knives, spoons and sometimes napkins for all the people that will be eating with me.

I need to set a plate, a cup, a fork, a knife, a spoon and a napkin at each place where someone will be sitting.

At each place where someone will sit, I place the fork on the left side of the plate, and I place the napkin, knife, spoon, and cup on the right side of the plate.

My mom or dad will be very happy with me for setting the table.

37

I Will Chew My Food Quietly at Mealtime

-Katie Eldean

Sometimes when I am eating I am told to quiet down while I chew.

Usually it is polite to keep my mouth closed so noises do not come out.

It is very unappetizing to hear or see the food in other peoples' mouths.

If I look around at the other people sitting with me, I will hopefully see their mouths closed, too.

At mealtime, I will take small bites and try to chew with my mouth closed.

38

Saying a Prayer at Mealtime

-Katie Eldean

Sometimes my family says a prayer before we eat our meal.

Prayers are a time when the whole family or one member shares their worries, thoughts, or thanks.

Prayers are usually a quiet time to praise God.

I will try to be quiet and keep my eyes closed when prayer is taking place.

I will try not talk loudly, interrupt, or open my eyes when my family says a prayer. My mom or dad will tell me when we are done.

Trying New Foods

-Nathan Vannoy

When I am eating, I may see a new kind of food that I have not tried before. I will not know what it tastes like unless I try some.

If somebody asks me to try the new food, I will try it to find out if I like it.

I may like to try new foods. Sometimes if I like it, I can have more.

If I do not like it, I will say "No thank you," and probably will not have to eat anymore.

If I do not try the new food, I will never know if I like it. I will try new foods before I say I do not like it.

Why I Eat Healthy

-Marci Martin

I like to eat healthy.

It is important for me to eat out of the five major food groups which include Meat, Dairy, Bread & Cereal, Vegetables, and Fruit.

I should eat from one of the food groups at least once a day so I stay healthy.

I will eat food that I know is good for me.

It makes me happy knowing I eat healthy to keep my body growing strong.

Chapter 5

Helping Around the House

Cleaning My Room

-Shelley Boes

Sometimes my room gets messy.

Sometimes when my room is messy I cannot find the things I need.

When my room gets messy, I need to clean it.

I pick up my toys and put them away.

I pick up my clothes and put them away neatly where they belong.

Mom and dad like to see my room clean.

Making My Bed

-Andy Veach

When I wake up in the morning I get out of bed.

I will try to straighten the sheets on my bed.

I will try to straighten the blankets on my bed.

I will try to place the pillows up at the top of my bed.

Then my bed is made.

Turn Off The Lights

-Tracie Taylor

I will try to remember to turn the lights off at the right times.

Sometimes when I am in a room, I like to have the lights on. I can see better with the lights on.

Sometimes when I walk out of the room, I should turn the lights off. If I am the only person in the room, when I walk out I will try to remember to turn off the lights.

If I turn the lights off, I will save money.

Mom and dad will be happy with me if I turn off the lights at the right times.

44

Turning Off The Lights

-Dan DeHommel

The lights allow me to see when it is dark.

The lights help me to see what I am doing.

The lights help others see what they are doing, too.

The lights are bright and sometimes hurt my eyes when I look at them.

I may turn the lights off when no one else is using them.

Vacuum Cleaner

-Jeff Burgess

I may like it when my family uses a vacuum cleaner.

Some people like it when the vacuum cleaner runs. Some people like the sound of the vacuum cleaner.

The vacuum cleaner makes my house clean. Most people like clean houses.

Most people like vacuum cleaners.

When do I get the mail?

-Claire Pape

Sometimes I get the mail.

I know the mail is here if I see the mail person put the mail in the mailbox.

Usually I do not see the mail person put mail in my mailbox.

Sometimes other people may get the mail from the mailbox.

Sometimes the mail person is not on time. Sometimes the mail person might have car trouble, or might be a little late.

Sometimes the mail person does not bring mail. On Sunday the mail does not come. Sometimes on holidays the mail does not come.

I will ask my mom and dad when I should go and get the mail.

My mom and dad can tell me when the mail is not going to come.

Chapter 6

Recess and Outdoor

May I pick the flowers?

-Angee Vredenburg

There are many colors, shapes, and sizes of flowers.

Some flowers smell nice.

Some flowers smell OK.

Sometimes I can pick flowers if I ask an adult first.

I might like to pick flowers.

Time to Rest

-Kristy Walton

It is fun to play.

Sometimes I run, jump, and yell when I play.

It is fun to yell when I am playing.

Sometimes when I am playing, I get too loud.

Sometimes my mom and dad tell me I am too loud. I might need to rest when I get too loud.

Sometimes I can eat a snack, take a nap, or watch a movie when I rest.

Why should I play outside?

-Kristyn Fleser

Playing outside is fun.

Sometimes when I play outside, I feel better.

Sometimes the outside makes me feel refreshed and excited.

Sometimes I can play on the toys, if there are some.

Usually, I can play with my friends. They like the outside too.

Sometimes I can swing on the swings.

Playing outside creates a better attitude.

Sometimes we can listen with our ears and hear the wind.

Playing outside maybe fun. When we play outside, the feeling can be awesome.

Chapter 7

All About School

Getting Ready in the Morning

-Joachim Weitgasser

When students have school they get up early, as they want to be at school before it starts.

Most people like to have clean faces and hands when they are at school. Sometimes they wash themselves in the morning.

I comb my hair and brush my teeth after I get up.

Sometimes I even take a shower in the morning because I will feel fresher. I want to smell good and look good.

When I meet other people, I usually want to smell good and look good.

After I wash myself, I put on my clothes. Usually I change my clothes every day.

Most people change their clothes every day. Sometimes my parents or guardians will tell me which clothes I should wear.

Most people like to eat a breakfast in the morning. Sometimes I eat breakfast before I wash and get dressed.

Sometimes I eat breakfast after I wash and get dressed.

I get up at the time my parents or guardians tell me. I wash myself, get dressed and eat breakfast. Then it is usually time to go to school.

How can I walk to school safely?

-Sarah Smeenge

My name is _____. I am in the first grade.

I go to _____ School. I live two blocks from school.

Usually when I leave my house in the morning, I walk on my driveway to the sidewalk.

There are a lot of things to look at outside, but I need to think about where I am going.

It is important to know the way to school. I need to know which way to walk.

I will get someone to help me at first until I know the way. My mom, dad, or a friend are people I could ask to help me with this. To be safe, I need to stop when the sidewalk ends because of a crossroad. Then I need to look for cars.

If I see a car that is close to me, I need to wait until the car goes by, then I can cross the street.

To be safe, I must also remember to only talk with people I know.

When I start walking to school, I must walk all the way to school. I must follow the rules for entering the school.

If I walk to school and pay attention to where I am going, I will get to school safely.

52

Riding the School Bus

-Valerie Lowing

Some children ride to school on a bus.

Usually the bus will pick me up in the morning and bring me to school.

Some children like riding the bus. They think it is fun.

Usually the bus will pick me up from school at the end of the day and bring me back home.

Sometimes I will not ride the bus. Mom or dad will tell me when I will not ride the bus.

Having a Substitute Teacher

-Bill Kremer

When I have a substitute teacher it gives me a chance to learn something from a new person.

Sometimes my regular teacher is gone. She may be away learning new ways to teach.

My substitute teacher will try to be as nice as my regular teacher. She may also be a little nervous. I may be a little nervous, too. It will be nice to make a new friend.

I will try to treat my substitute teacher like I treat my regular teacher. The substitute is trying, too. I will follow the rules of my regular teacher.

54

Listening to the Teacher

-Brit Strangways

It is good to listen to the teacher.

The teacher helps us learn.

When I have a question, I raise my hand and wait for the teacher to call on me.

I can listen when the teacher is teaching. I will try to listen to what the teacher is saying.

Sometimes we might have a substitute teacher. I can listen to the substitute teacher.

What should I do when the teacher is talking?

-Kelly Goward

I go to school almost every Monday, Tuesday, Wednesday, Thursday, and Friday.

There are many other children at school. In my classroom, the children usually sit at their desks.

When the teacher is talking to the class, the children are usually quiet. When someone wants to say something, they usually raise their hand and wait for the teacher to call on them.

When the teacher is talking to the class, I will try to be quiet and listen.

When I want to say something, I will try to remember to raise my hand and wait for the teacher to call on me.

The teacher will be happy if I try to be quiet and listen.

The teacher will be happy if I raise my hand before I talk.

Getting My Turn to Talk in Class

-Jamie Sabourin

There are many students in a classroom who like to talk at the same time.

It is hard for a teacher to hear one student talk if everyone else is talking, too.

When I want to talk to the teacher in class, I will usually raise my hand and sit quietly.

The teacher will usually call on me to talk if I raise my hand in the air. I may have to wait for a turn to talk.

If I want to talk to the teacher during class, I will raise my hand and wait for the teacher to call on me.

Staying Calm in Class

-Tyler Steketee

Most classes are fun.

If I stay calm in class, I will learn more.

The more I learn, the more I can do.

If I stay calm, my teacher will be happy and will teach me new things.

Learning new things is fun most of the time.

Staying calm in class will help me understand the teacher.

How to Ask for Help

-Jackie Leese

Sometimes, children have school work they cannot figure out.

Sometimes, when children cannot figure out school work, they get frustrated.

I will try to stay calm.

Children need to ask their teachers for extra help if they need it.

It is OK to ask for extra help from teachers.

If I need help on schoolwork, I will ask for it.

Asking a Question in Class

-Katie Wood

Sometimes in class I have a question.

When I want to ask a question, I raise my hand and wait until the teacher calls my name. When the teacher calls my name, that means it is my turn to ask my question.

I will put my hand down and ask the teacher my question.

The teacher will do her best to answer my question.

I will try to listen carefully to her answer.

Sometimes the teacher will not have an answer. That is okay too.

I will try to wait patiently and quietly until my teacher calls on me to ask my question.

Could you please repeat that?

-Kristy Moseler

When I do not understand something that is said to me, I need to ask that person to repeat what they said.

I can look at them and say, "Could you please repeat that? I don't understand."

They will repeat the question so I can understand it better.

I can now answer the question correctly because I understand.

What am I supposed to do at recess?

-Sarah Smeenge

Usually I have recess most of the days I go to school. Sometimes one recess is in the morning, and the other is in the afternoon.

Recess is a time that I can go outside. I can walk and run around. I can also talk out loud.

When I am in class I often need to sit still, be quiet, and do my work. I listen to my teacher.

When I go outside, I can talk and move around. I can choose what equipment I want to play on. Usually there will be things to climb, slide down, or swing on.

I can also play a game if I want to with some of the other students. Sometimes I play tag or baseball.

Recess is a good time to get rid of some of my extra energy that builds up while I am sitting quietly in class.

When recess is over, I may feel ready to sit down quietly in my classroom again. I am ready to listen and learn. It is fun and helpful to have recess.

Assemblies

-Amy Kovach

There may be times during the school year when my schedule changes. Sometimes I will go to an assembly.

Many students think most assemblies are fun.

If I have an assembly, my teacher or another adult will tell me when it is time to go and where to go.

When I have an assembly, there are a lot of people there. Usually it is not just my class.

Sometimes we go to an assembly to listen to someone speak. If that is the type of assembly that I am going to, I will sit where I am asked to sit. I will try to be quiet.

I will try to listen to what the speaker says. Usually I will clap when the speaker is finished speaking. I will try to clap when everyone else claps.

There are times when we go to spirit assemblies. This assembly involves the whole school. Sometimes at these assemblies it is OK to cheer and be noisy.

When I go to these assemblies, I will try to watch what other students are doing so I know what I am supposed to do. If everyone is cheering it is OK if I cheer.

Sometimes when people are standing, I should stand up.

Usually if people are clapping, I clap my hands.

If someone is talking in the microphone, I try to stay quiet so I can hear what they are saying.

When I go to an assembly, I will try and have fun.

63

When the Fire Alarm Goes Off

-Erin Klooster

Sometimes as I sit in class I hear a buzzing alarm go off. The alarm means we are having a fire drill.

A fire drill gives students a chance to practice for a real fire. Usually there is not really a fire.

My teacher waits for me to line up with my class at the door. I walk quietly down the hall with my class.

I walk outside and wait until my teacher says that we can go back inside.

The fire drill is over when my teacher leads us back inside.

64

What do I do in a fire drill?

-Crissy DeWeerd

Sometimes at school we have fire drills. They are only practice. Usually fire drills only last a short time.

Usually, there is not a real fire. I have to practice just in case.

When I hear the alarm, I quietly get up from my seat when my teacher tells me to.

I stand in line with my class and we walk outside with our teacher.

When the fire drill is done, I can go back to my classroom.

65

Afternoon Announcements

-Scott Kohsel

Each day we listen to afternoon announcements. I try to be quiet and listen.

It is important to be quiet.

I will try to sit and pay attention. What they say is important to me. I will try to listen so that I know what is going to happen.

That is why I listen to the afternoon announcements.

Why should I do homework?

-Felicia Kinde

During the week, I usually go to school.

While I am at school, my teacher might assign homework for me to do. Sometimes I want to do something else instead.

If I do my homework, I will probably learn new things and maybe practice what I have already done.

When I am told to do my homework, I will try do it the best that I can.

Chapter 8

Getting Around

Escalators

-Dan Wyma

Escalators can be found in many stores.

I can use them for going up or down.

Escalators are very safe when used in the right way.

I must make sure I know which way the escalator is going.

After I step onto the escalator, I hang on to the railing until the moving stairs slide under the floor in front of me.

When the stairs slide under the floor. The floor is not moving.

Many people think escalators are fun to use.

Riding in a Car

-Kristen Dressel

When I need to go away, I usually ride in a car.

I ride in cars with people I know, like my family. Sometimes my parents or teachers tell me it is O. K. to ride with them.

I open the car door when I get in the car.

I always wear my seat belt because it keeps me safe.

It helps the driver concentrate when I sit quietly in the car. I need to keep my hands to myself. I need to talk quietly when someone is driving.

When I am riding in a car, I keep the door closed. The driver stops the car and tells me when it is O.K. to open the door and get out.

Riding in the Car

-Vicki L. DeLang

Sometimes, I ride in the car and travel to other places.

When I get in the car, I open the door of the car and sit down.

After sitting down, I grab my seat belt strap, put it over my lap, and connect the two seat belt ends.

When I ride in the car, I sit still and watch the scenery.

Sometimes, it seems like the car is close to other cars, but I am safe. The person driving is controlling the car and knows what to do.

70

Wearing Seat Belts

-Kristen Oberg

When I get into a car I fasten my seat belt. It keeps me safe.

My seat belt may seem tight or uncomfortable but it keeps me safe.

Every time I get into an automobile I grab the seat belt strap, find the handle, and push it into the holder. When I hear a CLICK sound, I know my seat belt is fastened. I know I'm safe.

I am safe in my seat belt. That is why I wear a seat belt.

71

Why do I have to Wear a Seat Belt?

-Jessica Maier

Usually when my mom or my dad go to the store or go away, they usually go by car.

Sometimes I go with them. They always want me to wear my seat belt. My mom and dad ask me to wear my seat belt. They love me and they do not want me to get hurt. Sometimes a car bumps into another car. It is important for me to wear my seat belt, so I won't fall out of my seat.

I will always buckle up.

Chapter 9

Community Helpers

Going Through the Car Wash

-Suzanne Spoelhof

Sometimes the car gets dirty. The snow or rain or other things splash up from the road. The car looks dirty.

One way my mom or dad wash the car is by taking it to the car wash.

Car washes can be different. Sometimes, I might get out of the car and watch the car go through the car wash. Sometimes, I stay in the car with my mom or dad. We ride through the car wash.

The car goes in the car wash. The water comes down to rinse the car off. I will stay dry because I am in the car and it will protect me. I am safe.

Next the soap comes down. The soap gets the car clean like the soap I use in the bath gets me clean.

Next, two or three sets of brushes scrub the car. They are noisy.

I will try not to be afraid of the brushes because I know I am safe. The brushes are outside the car and I am inside.

After the car is scrubbed, more water comes down to rinse all the soap off.

The water stops. The car moves through some long cloths like towels hanging from the ceiling. These cloths dry off the car.

The water gets blown off the car by big hot air blowers. The blowers are noisy.

I am still safe.

The car moves through more cloths hanging from the ceiling.

The car wash is over. The car is clean.

Going to Church

-Randy Riksen

Sometimes people go to church.

Some people think going to church is fun. Sometimes during church, I am able to sing. When I sing, I will be sure I can hear the person next to me.

Sometimes I will sit next to someone I do not know. It is polite to say, "Hello," to them when they say, "Hello," to me.

It is respectful to sit quietly while the pastor or someone up front is speaking to the congregation. There may be a lot of people in the congregation. If I am asked to speak I should speak quietly so I do not disturb other people.

How to Sit Still During Prayer

-Melissa Schipper

I sit in church on Sunday.

The minister talks to me and many other people.

When it is time to pray, the minister usually will say, "Let us pray."

I bow my head, close my eyes, and put my hands together.

When the minister is praying, I will try to be quiet and sit still.

When the minister is done praying, he says, "Amen."

Sometimes the minister does not say, "Amen." My mom and dad will let me know we are done.

After the minister is done praying, I open my eyes and look at the minister.

Sometimes someone other than the minister prays. I will try to act the same as when the minister is praying.

I will try to sit quietly when someone is praying.

Going to the Library

-Kelly Rodgers

The library is a quiet place.

I can get books to read.   Sometimes I can rent videos or read magazines.

The library is a place where I can study, do my homework, or look up information that I might need to know for class.

When I am at the library, I will try to be quiet.

If I have a question or need to talk to someone I should *whisper* quietly.

If I find a book that I like, I can read it at the library, or I can bring it home.

If I want to bring it home, I must go to the front and give the clerk my books.

The clerk will check them out so I can bring them home.

The clerk writes a date in the front cover. This is the date I have to bring the books back.

Sometimes I need help finding a book that I want. I can go to the front desk or find a person that works at the library to help me. I can ask them to help me. Usually they will be happy to help me find a book.

Why do I get my hair cut?

-Amy Wolkowitz

My hair is constantly growing.

Sometimes hair needs to be cut.

Barbers are trained to cut hair. Usually it does not hurt when the barber cuts my hair.

I will try to remember that it is a safe to get my hair cut.

Chapter 10

Restaurants and Shopping

An Eating Experience

-Sam Rodriguez

Sometimes I go out to eat with my family. I may have a fun time when we go out to eat.

Sometimes we go to a big restaurant. Sometimes we go to a small restaurant.

When we go out to eat, I will try to be on my best behavior.

Usually there are other people eating at the restaurant. Sometimes I am seated by a waitress or waiter.

I usually pick what I want to eat from a menu. I will try to be polite to the waitress or waiter.

Sometimes I order my food at a counter.

Waiting for a Table

-Janet Williams

When I go to a restaurant, there might not be a table that is ready for me.

There may be other people who are also waiting for a table.

Some of those people may have gotten to the restaurant before I did, so I will have to wait for my turn.

Sometimes there is a list of people waiting for a table. I can put my last name or the last name of someone I will be eating with on the list.

When the name is called that I wrote down, it is my turn and there will be a table for me.

Going Out to Eat

-Denise Andringa

Most people like to go out to eat.

When people go out to eat, they may get dressed up, depending on where they are going. Mom and dad will tell me if I have to get dressed up.

Sometimes I may have to wait in line before I can get seated. That is OK because I will be seated.

When I am seated, I will look at the menu to see what I want to eat and drink. I will tell Mom and dad.

When the waiter or waitress comes to ask what I would like to eat, I will tell her what I would like.

It may take a while for the dinner to come but we will get our dinner. Sometimes we get the drinks before the meal.

Talking in a Restaurant

-Carrie Rikkers

Sometimes my parents or relatives like to go out to eat.

Sometimes they take me along. It can be fun to eat in a restaurant.

My parents or relatives will let me know what kind of restaurant we will go to.

If it is a fancy restaurant, we wear nice clothes.

In a restaurant, I will try to talk quietly. Other people like to talk to the people at their table without interruptions.

When I talk softly, the other people I am sitting with can still hear me.

I should try to talk softly, so people will not get upset and leave.

I like to make people happy, so I will try my best to talk quietly.

When is it OK to eat with my fingers?

-Carrie Rikkers

Sometimes my parents like to take me out to eat.

When we are at the restaurant, they may show us to our table and give us menus.

My parents will help me order my food. They know what food is affordable and good to eat.

When I get my food, I should use my silverware.

It is O.K. to use my fingers to pick up food that falls in my lap. I can pick it up and set it on the edge of my plate.

Sometimes it is also O.K. to use my fingers if my parents say so. I can ask if it would be O.K. to use my fingers.

If it is not right to use my fingers, the silverware is the best thing for me to use.

Eating in a Restaurant

-Molly Hayes

Going to a restaurant is different than eating at home. There are other people eating there, too.

I sit at a table and read the menu. It has lots of foods listed on it. I will try to use my best manners when around other people.

The waitress asks me what I would like to eat. I tell her what I have chosen and she goes to get it. Sometimes the wait is long. I may get really hungry while I am waiting.

I will try to wait patiently for my food to come.

When my food comes there might be different plates that it comes on. That is O.K. too. The silverware near my plate is for different things. I will use silverware for eating.

When I have finished eating, the waitress will bring me a bill for the food that I ordered. Sometimes there are even little mints with the bill.

When I have paid my bill, I leave the restaurant.

Going Shopping

-Carrie Rikkers

When I go shopping with my parents, they already know what to buy. Sometimes they make a list, other times they remember what we need.

When they make a list, I can look at the list and try to find the items on the shelves.

Sometimes I want a special treat. It is okay to ask my parents for a treat if I see something I would like to have.

My parents know what is best for me. They will tell me if it is all right to get a treat. They may say, "No," or "Maybe another time."

Getting New Shoes

-Jamie Kinder

I wear shoes on my feet to keep them warm and protect them.

Sometimes my shoes get old and wear out. I sometimes need new shoes.

Sometimes I go to a shoe store to get new shoes.

A man or a woman will help me find new shoes that fit my feet.

I will try to be quiet in the shoe store.

Getting new shoes can be fun.

Chapter 11

Understanding the Weather

Hail

-Suzanne Speolhof

Hail is a part of nature.

Hail is little pieces of ice that fall like rain.

The sound of hail hitting things may be scary.

Hail can make loud noises. I am safe inside.

Rainy Days

-Jamie Kinder

The weather isn't always nice.

Sometimes it rains.

When it rains water falls from the sky.

Sometimes it is okay to go out in the rain. I will ask an adult if it is safe to go outside.

I should wear a jacket when I go out in the rain. A jacket will keep my clothes dry.

How to Make A Snow Angel

-Hank Kulfeldt

When winter comes, snow falls. The snow is wet and very cold.

Some children like to play in the snow.

Sometimes the snow tickles when it lands on my skin.

Sometimes I am able to play in the snow. Sometimes I make snow angles. I might like to make snow angels. Snow angels are pretty.

When the snow falls, I wait until morning and ask my mom or dad to help me put my winter clothes on.

First, I put on my clothes so that I will stay warm. Sometimes, my winter clothes help me stay healthy.

I put on my snowsuit, boots, hat, and mittens. Sometimes I put on a scarf.

Sometimes my mom or dad will help me put on my winter clothes.

Sometimes, I walk outside into the cold air. I can look for a spot of snow close to the house away from the road to make my snow angel. I make sure that I am away from the trees and bushes so I will be safe.

Sometimes I can make a snow angel.

1. I sit in the snow.

2. I can lay back so that I am looking straight up at the sky.

3. I can move my arms through the snow, touching my hips and then making my hands meet in the snow above my head.

4. I move my legs from side to side and then I stop.

5. I sit straight up.

6. I stand up and turn around to look at the angel I just made.

My snow angel is pretty.

Thunderstorms

-Jamie Kinder

Thunderstorms make a lot of noise.

The noise can be loud. Sometimes the noise might hurt my ears.

I cannot see the thunder. I am safe inside.

Thunderstorms usually don't last very long. When the storm is over the noises will stop.

What to Do When it Rains

-Jenny Friesema

Rain comes and goes unexpectedly. If I want to know if it will rain today or tomorrow, I can listen to the weather report on the radio or on the television.

If I am outside when it begins to rain, I will find a safe place to go inside. If I stay outside, I will probably get wet.

If it starts to rain while I am at home or school, I try to remember if I left any of my belongings outside. If something is outside, it will get wet in the rain.

If I did leave something outside, I will ask for permission to quickly go and get it. After I get it, I will bring it inside.

90

When the Lights Go Out

-Charlie Frayman

Sometimes when there is a thunderstorm, the lights may go out.

Thunderstorms may seem scary. It might be scary if the lights go out.   Sometimes when the lights go out, they might be off for a few seconds, a few minutes, or a few hours. To help myself I can close my eyes or ask for a hug to comfort me.

Other people around me might be frightened, too. Someone by me might need a hug, too.

Thunderstorms are OK

-COURTNEY RICHTER

I think flowers are pretty.

I like green grass, too.

If the flowers and the grass didn't get water they might die and look ugly. One way they get water is from rain that falls from the clouds.

Sometimes clouds make a bright flash and a loud bang when it rains. This is lightening and thunder.

Sometimes the wind blows real strong and I can hear the trees blowing outside.

If I look out the window I can see the water falling on the flowers and the trees.

It's okay if there is lightening and thunder when it's raining.

I know the flowers and the grass will look pretty and make everybody happy.

Chapter 12

Holidays, Vacations, Recreation

Valentine's Day

-Anna Canales

Valentine Day is February 14.

On Valentine Day I can show someone that I love them.

There are many things I can give to a person I care about. I can give candy, flowers, or even a card.

I can make a card out paper. I can draw big red hearts on the card.

I can make a Valentine card for each person that I love.

Valentine Day is a day to show people that I care about them.

The National Anthem

-Janet Williams

Sometimes the National Anthem is played or sung.

It is a song that is special to our country.

Many people think that our country is special. They think that the National Anthem is special.

When the song is played, I will stand up. There might even be a flag near me that I can look at while I listen to the song.

If I am wearing a hat, I take it off until the song is done.

The Fourth of July Fireworks

-Scott Potter

Every year I have a birthday. Even the country I live in has a birthday. It is on July 4.

For my birthday I have cake and open presents. When my country has a birthday, I sometimes celebrate with fireworks.   I watch fireworks outside or on TV.

Sometimes fireworks make loud noises and have bright lights.

The fireworks are safe. If I am frightened, I will hug my mom and dad. Hugging mom or dad might help me feel more safe.

I will let an adult light the fireworks so that I will be safe.

When I Swim

-David Albrecht

When I swim on hot days, the water will cool me off.

Sometimes it is fun to go swimming with my family and friends.

Swimming is a form of exercise that will make me stronger.

When I swim, I will wear my life jacket so that I am safe.

I will always have an adult watch me when I swim.

Vacations

-Michelle Huyser

Sometimes I have time off from school. This is called a vacation.

Vacations are a time when schools are closed.

It is ok to be home on a weekday when I have a vacation.

Vacations are usually fun.

Sometimes vacations are one or two days. Sometimes vacations are for one or two weeks. Sometimes vacations are longer.

After the vacation is done the school opens.   I usually can go back to school.

Going To The Zoo

-Shelley Boes

Going to the zoo can be fun.

When I go to the zoo I see many different animals.

Animals are kept in cages for my safety.

I will keep my hands outside the cages.

The zoo is a fun place to learn about animals.

Going To See A Play

-Linda Hurd

Sometimes mom and dad will want to see a play.

A play is when people get dressed up in costumes and act out a story.

Sometimes a play will make me laugh. These plays are called comedies.

Sometimes a play will be serious. These plays are called dramas.

I can only talk during a play if it is very important.

I will try to pay attention to the play.

I will try to be quiet. Other people around me are trying to watch the play.

Day Spent At The Ballpark

-Beth Cigler

Sometimes mom and dad take me to a baseball game.

The game could be a high school or major league game.

Sometimes the stadium is far away. It might take a long time to get there. I will try to be patient. I play car games until we get there.

I get out of the car. I walk to the stadium.

I find my seat. If I have to go to the bathroom, I will tell Mom or Dad. They will take me to a bathroom.

Sometimes I get souvenirs.

I can ask Mom or Dad to buy me a souvenir. Sometimes they say, "Yes," and sometimes they say, "No." Either way, I try to be happy.

When I get hungry, I tell Mom or Dad. They might get me something to eat. They might ask me to wait.

The game usually lasts 9 innings. If it starts to rain, the game might be postponed or canceled.

When the game is over, we get in the car and go home.

Sometimes we stop to get something to eat.

Playing Video Games

-Beth Cigler

Sometimes I play with video games.

Sometimes I have many games to choose from. Not everyone has a lot of video games to play with.

I might play by myself, or I might have someone play with me.

We take turns playing the video game.

Sometimes I win the video game and sometimes I lose.

It is OK if I lose. I will try to be a *good sport*.. A *good sport* is someone who plays fair. A *good sport* stays calm if he loses.

Chapter 13

The Social Story Kit

The Social Story Kit
-Carol Gray

Getting Started

Social Stories describe social situations in terms of relevant social cues, and often define appropriate responses. Social stories present social information to students with autism, while minimizing the social aspects of teacher/student interactions involved in instruction. In this way, social information is presented as clearly as possible, with limited interference from the social interactions involved in traditional teaching.

Social Stories are written in response to individual student needs. These needs may be identified through:

1) observations of situations which are difficult for the student;

2) the student's responses to questions about social situations which indicate the student is "misreading" a given situation; and/or

3) social skills assessments and curriculums.

Based on identified needs, social stories may:

1) describe any situation in terms of the relevant social cues and/or correct responses in a non-threatening format;

2) personalize or emphasize social skills covered in any social skills training program;

3) translate goals (possibly written by students) into understandable steps;

4) explain the "fictional" qualities of commercial stories/movies/etc., identifying realistically appropriate from inappropriate interactions depicted in those stories;

5) teach routines, as well as helping students to accommodate changes in routine or "forgetting";

6) teach academic material in a realistic, social "backdrop", assisting students in relating learned skills to real situations; and/or

7) address a wide variety of behaviors, including aggression, fear, and obsessions and compulsions.

Social Stories are usually written by parents or professionals. Experience with social stories indicates they are most likely to be effective with students functioning at or above the trainable mentally impaired range of intellectual functioning. Reading ability is not necessarily required. Through the use of accompanying audio cassette tapes, social stories have been effective with non-readers.

To begin writing a social story:

First, target and observe a situation which is difficult for a student. Social stories include those things which usually occur, and some possible changes in routine. Watch for those factors you can see and hear, and take plenty of notes. Also imagine those aspects of the situation which you are *not* observing. Record these as possible variations. Using the *Social Story Information* form is helpful when gathering information for a social story (Appendix A: Social Story Forms). For example, is gym always on Tuesday at 10:30, or is it sometimes canceled? Do the students always line up in the same order? Should a student do something different when lining up for lunch versus lining up to go home? Ask plenty of questions as part of the observation. In this way each story is honest and realistic, describing variations as part of the routine.

Remember there are two valid perceptions of the situation you are observing: yours, and that of the student with autism. Through observation of the student in the situation, try to determine what may be motivating his/her current responses. Does the student seem fearful? Does it seem like he/she is more sensitive to the situation than the other students? What does the student report about the situation? *It is the student's perspective which will guide you in knowing which aspects of a situation you will be writing about. The student's perspective determines the focus of the social story.*

Social stories are comprised of three basic types of sentences: **descriptive, perspective, and directive sentences**. Descriptive sentences objectively define where a situation occurs, who is involved, what they are doing, and why. Perspective sentences describe the reactions and feelings of others in a given situation. Directive sentences are individualized statements of desired responses. They often follow descriptive sentences, telling a student what is expected as a response to a given cue or situation. Directive sentences often begin with "I can try to...", "I will try..." or "I will work on...". What follows is a sample of each type of sentence:

Sometimes a person says, "I changed my mind" (descriptive). This means they had one idea, but now they have a new idea (perspective). There are many situations where a person may say, "I changed my mind" (descriptive). I will work on staying calm when someone changes their mind (directive). It is important to try to stay calm (descriptive). This keeps everyone safe (descriptive).

A good formula to follow for most stories is to write a total of at *least three to five* descriptive, perspective and/or control sentences for every directive sentence in a story. This is the Social Story Ratio:

<u>0 - 1 directive sentences</u> = SOCIAL STORY RATIO
2 - 5 descriptive and/or perspective sentences

The most common mistake in writing social stories is too few descriptive and perspective sentences, and too many directive sentences. The more descriptive and perspective sentences there are in a story, and the fewer directive sentences, the more opportunity there is for an individual to determine his/her own new responses to a situation. Take time to carefully describe what people do, and why. Keep in mind, though, that for some students a totally descriptive story will be confusing, leaving a student at a loss for what is expected. These students will need directive statements in the story.

A word of caution regarding directive sentences. Avoid using statements that are inflexible, or that require absolute compliance for a student to feel successful as a learner. For example, statements that begin with "I can...", "I will..." or "I should..." leave little room for error. These may result in a student feeling pressured to comply with specific responses right from the start.

Guidelines for first time social story writers:

- When writing a social story, write well within a student's comprehension level, using vocabulary and print size appropriate for a student's ability.

- Usually, social stories are written in the first person and the present tense, as though the student is describing events as they take place.

- Social stories may be written in the future tense, to describe an upcoming situation to make it seem less threatening. Relating aspects of the anticipated event to a more familiar event, setting, or activity may be helpful.

- Use illustrations carefully. Illustrations may enhance the meaning of a social story, especially for young not-yet readers. Simple, clear stick figures illustrations may be the best choice. As a general rule, avoid illustrations with too many details, as they may be misleading to a student who tends to interpret illustrated information literally. Photographs may be useful, but be aware that the background may contain unintended extraneous information.

- Social stories often describe one aspect or one step of a social situation per page, to further define the separate steps of a situation. Use only a few sentences per page. This also allows the story to be used as a curriculum story, or an interactive story (two variations of social stories described in the next section).

- Avoid terms like *always,* instead using terms like *usually* or *sometimes* when writing a social story.

- State directive sentences positively, describing desired responses instead of describing problem behaviors.

Variations

Checklist Social Stories

Checklist stories are social stories which actively involve the student in practicing certain skills without the confusion of the actual situation surrounding them. Often they are written to teach a sequence of activities. One example: Each page of a story describes a step of a daily routine. Each step of the routine is described on its own sheet of paper. At the end of the story, is a checklist of the steps comprising the routine, and the student "checks off" each completed step contained in the story.

By removing any selected page of the story, a step of the routine is eliminated. First, the student is given the opportunity to remove a page, causing the character in the story to "forget" a step of the routine - which the student indicates when he reaches the final checklist and does **not** place a check by the missing step. The character receives "help" from the student as the student replaces the missing step and checks off the missing step.

Later, staff may "pull" a step from the story in the same way (by removing one of the pages). By paying close attention, the student identifies the forgotten step as he completes the checklist. The student must now request help from the teacher to replace the missing step into the story.

Through this process, a student learns to handle "forgetting" by asking for help first within the safer, less stressful context of reading a story. By reading the story several times, the student learns the routine described by the story as well, and may identify and handle forgotten steps more appropriately when actually completing the targeted routine.

With each step of a routine listed on it's own page, checklist stories are easily used as a "real life" sequencing activity. Eliminate the page numbers in the story, and place the pages in random order. The student tries to arrange the pages in the correct order.

Curriculum Stories

Many students with autism have difficulty applying academic skills to "real life" situations. The value or impact of a social story may be expanded by using a format to allow the insertion of a variety of related academic pages into the story, without changing the story line. The result is a curriculum story.

Curriculum stories incorporate various aspects of the academic curriculum into the social story, and keep social stories, (which may need to be reread a few times to be effective) interesting. Social stories can be written so curriculum pages can be easily inserted throughout the story. One example: after a description and photograph of a student in line, a math insert may ask the student to count the number of students (or the number of girls, boys, or smiles) standing in line in the photograph on the previous page.

Academic curriculum inserts can address a student's specific academic objectives, encouraging application of writing, math, or guessing skills, for example. Curriculum stories use targeted social situations (or any situation) from a student's specific life experiences as a "backdrop" to demonstrate the functional application and relationships between academic concepts and everyday life.

A Generic Social Story

It may be difficult for a teacher to keep up with the demand for social stories. One solution: the teacher writes a generic story, an outline, and the support staff individualize and bring it to the final copy. Generic social stories are useful in providing support staff with the needed confidence to write a social story. With a generic story as a starting point, it is easier to write a final individualized story than to write a social story from "scratch." (Appendix B: Generic Social Story)

A generic story provides direction for writing an individualized story for a student. Generic stories are written in a **descriptive** format. Parts of the story may be deleted or altered to describe a student's specific environment and situation. Also, **directive** statements are often added to individualize the story.

Other Social Story Variations

In addition to checklist, curriculum, and generic stories, there are additional basic variations of social stories which can be used to address other skills and situations. These are briefly described in this section.

Goal stories incorporate a habit associated with success - goal setting - into social stories. The social story is written minus the directive sentences. The directive sentences are provided by the student, for example, following a description of a situation in a social story the student completes the directive sentence, *"I will_____,"* which becomes the student's goal for the next time the situation occurs.

Judgment stories provide a wide variety of visual and functional cues to assist a student in making a needed judgment. For example, to assist a student who is singing louder than other members of a choir, a judgment story might include statements like, *"Volume is a word that means how loud someone sings. A good way to sing with the right volume is to make sure I can hear the person singing next to me. I can tell when it is time for a solo. People who have a solo sing alone. A person singing a solo has the microphone."*

Stories addressing aggression are highly descriptive and positively state desired responses. By carefully observing the student in the situation, it is often possible to determine the factors resulting in aggression. These stories carefully and thoroughly describe the situation, and provide positive directive statements to indicate desired responses.

Stories addressing fears are highly descriptive, and include visual descriptions of when the situation begins and ends. These stories describe factors which may be resulting in fearful response. It is also important to respect the student's fearful response, avoiding statements like *"There's no need to be afraid of..."*.

Stories addressing "obsessions" and "compulsions" matter-of-factly describe skills and/or situations where a target behavior occurs. Extensive observation may reveal the behavior is more a response to a misunderstanding than a desire to perform a behavior repeatedly, or in a specific rigid manner. For example, a student consistently and repeatedly erases her written work, writing the same letter and erasing it several times. As a result, she often erases holes in her paper. Careful observation indicates she is trying to write letters which are identical to typewritten letters. As a result, a social story is written for her which assures her that written words look different from typewritten words, and that it is okay for written words to look slightly different every time they are written.

Question and answer stories demonstrate the relationship between questions and answers. For example, a common question, "Mom, cookie?" is followed by a step by step description of Mom's possible responses. Questions can be used as titles for stories, followed by a general descriptive answer, for example, "What will we do at Disneyland?"

Media stories describe and/or discuss the confusing or ambiguous aspects of cartoons, stories, and other media.

Group stories are written for an entire group of students, and may contain an individualized directive sentence completed in a fill-in-the-blank format. For example, a group story written to prepare a class for an upcoming assembly describes the assembly and ends with each student's directive sentence, "At the assembly I will try to_____."

Recognizing the number of possible topics for social stories is equal only to the number of students and possible skills and situations, the above list is not to be considered all-inclusive.

Presenting a Social Story

The considerations given to the individual student and situation when writing a social story are equally important in presenting the story. In this section, a few of the most common accommodations used when presenting social stories are described.

A student's attention span, reading ability and comprehension skills will largely determine how words are presented on each page. For some students, a social story in standard size print, written from the top to the bottom of each page, will be easy to understand. Other students may need enlarged print, a few sentences to each page, or other accommodations to read and comprehend a story. To further define the separate steps of a situation, social stories often describe one aspect or one step of a social situation per page. This also allows the story to be used as a curriculum story, or a checklist story.

To focus attention on the written words, black construction paper is often used as a background to the written portion of a story. Each concept could be displayed on it's own black piece of construction paper. Experience indicates the use of black construction paper with one concept per page is often effective with young students interested in words.

For some students, especially young students or students who cannot read independently, making a audio cassette tape to accompany a story may be helpful. Read the story aloud into a cassette recorder and ring a bell or other signal to indicate when to turn each page. Teach the student how to use a cassette player along with the printed story.

For students who love to watch videotapes, or who can not read independently, placing a story on videotape may be effective. To place a story on video cassette, film each page. Allow enough time for the student to read each page. If the story is read aloud onto the videotape while filming, it will allow two options - for the story to be read to the student (volume on), or for the student to read the story himself (volume off). Videotaped sequences of the situation the story describes may be edited onto the videotape, spliced between the written sections of the story.

Implementing and Monitoring a Social Story

Implementing and monitoring a social story requires as much, if not more, care and consideration as gathering information, writing, and presenting the story. Listed in this section are guidelines and ideas for introducing, reviewing, and monitoring the effectiveness of a social story.

Take care to involve the expertise of others. Establish the cooperation, understanding, and support of those people in the target situation who are critical to a student's success. Prior to introducing the story to the student, distribute tentative copies of the story to others for revisions. This can catch inaccuracies, increase the details in a story, and save you and the student needless distress. *Involving the ideas and feedback of others in the final draft of the story is well worth the extra time it requires*

When introducing a story for the first time, begin with a quiet place with minimal distractions. It may be helpful to sit at the student's side, slightly back from where the student is sitting. The focus should be on the story, minimizing staff involvement as much as possible. The idea is to place the student in *direct contact with the information in the story.*

Keeping everyone informed as to the purpose and procedures surrounding a social story is important. Several ideas may be useful here. After sharing the story with the student, have the student show the story to others involved in the situation depicted in the story. By having others read the story aloud with the student present, the student quickly learns everyone has the same information and expectations. Also, those involved in the student's success in learning a new response to a situation clearly understand their role, and may refer to the story to assist the student when he/she encounters difficulty in the target situation. In addition, you may want to complete the *Social Story Implementation Plan* form and distribute copies to those involved in the target situation (Appendix A: Social Story Forms). Consistency among all involved can directly impact the effectiveness of the story and the student's progress.

Develop a consistent review schedule for the story. Many parents and professionals have found reading a story once a day, and perhaps just before the target situation, works well. Listen to the student for cues as to an appropriate review schedule. If a student indicates he/she "doesn't need to read it" on a given day, it can be "skipped" for a day. It is helpful to establish with the student, though, that you may ask that the story be read at another time. After a student gains independence from a story, instead of placing it in storage, keep it visible and accessible to the student as a reference. Many students may pride in keeping notebooks containing "mastered" stories, and they often review them on their own.

Once a story is part of a student's routine, continually monitor it's effectiveness. Careful observation may yield important information regarding which parts of a story are abstract or confusing. If this is the case, rewriting those sections may improve the student's performance. To assist a student as he/she gains independence, you may decide to eliminate some of the directive statements in the story. To "keep tabs" on a student's progress, the *Social Story Report* form is helpful (Appendix A: Social Story Forms).

Putting it All Together: The Social Story Quiz

To summarize this kit and to apply some of the concepts, take the short quiz in Appendix C. The quiz is intended to apply many of the guidelines for writing social stories. The answers are listed at the end of the quiz.

Appendix A: Social Story Forms

Teachers and consultants involved in extensive use of social stories may find the approach to be somewhat overwhelming: social stories can take time to write (especially at first), and monitoring several social stories requires organization. Use of Social Story Forms, included in this kit, minimize the time required to develop and monitor a social story.

The first form, *Social Stories Information*, structures observations and assists in gathering important information.   Whenever a situation is targeted for a student, one of these forms is used to record information needed to write the story. A completed Social Story Information form helps to ensure that all the information needed to write a social story has been gathered.

The second form, the *Social Story Implementation Plan* , is used to record a plan regarding instruction and review schedules surrounding a social story. Copies of this form may be distributed to all staff members who are involved with the student. This also provides a record of the methods and support materials selected for use with each story; information which may be useful in developing and implementing future stories.

The third form, *Social Story Report,* assists in keeping a record of a student's progress or difficulties with a social story. It is helpful for consultants trying to keep track of several students in different settings. As well as providing an efficient means of communication between a consultant and teacher, this form may also be valuable as a reference in the future.

Social Story Information

General Information

Name_____ School Year _____

Grade_____ Teacher_____ School_____

General Academic Information:
Reading Level:_____
Comprehension:_____
Math:_____

Interests/Special Abilities:
_____
_____
_____

Day / Time for: Art_____   Music_____   Phys Ed_____

P.T._____   O.T. _____   Speech _____

Other(s)_____

Names of a few classmates/ friends_____

Other general information _____

_____

Observation Notes

Targeted situation:_____

Time?_____   Day(s)?_____   til (date) _____

General description of targeted situation: _____

_____

Child's current response: _____   Always?_____

Desired response: _____

Teacher(s) attribute the response to: _____

Parents attribute the response to: _____

Child attributes the response to: _____

Date /notes of first observation: Date:____/____/____   Day:_____   Time:_____

Notes:_____

_____

_____

_____

_____

_____

Social Story Implementation Plan

Name:_____   Date_____

Title of Story_____

Story format: Printed story_____   Story and audio cassette_____   Story on videocassette_____

Suggested Implementation: **Begin implementing story on _____/_____/_____**

1. To introduce the story_____
_____
_____
_____

2. Review schedule _____
_____
_____
_____

3. Monitoring responses _____
_____
_____
_____

Progress review dates: _____/_____/_____;   _____/_____/_____;   _____/_____/_____

Suggested Fading Procedure: _____fading by re-writing   _____re-vising review schedule
_____decreasing verbal or other cues   _____other

Support Materials and Activities:

_____revise posted classroom schedule   _____story bookmark(s)
_____revise, modify written classroom rules   _____Reminder sign
_____"Keep Me Posted "notes   _____story passes
_____Story folder   _____Daily Oral Language (D.O.L.)
_____Social Calendar/Goals   _____Other

Describe:_____
_____
_____

_____

_____

_____

_____

_____

_____

_____

_____

Date /notes of second observation: Date:____/____/____   Day:_____Time:_____
Notes:_____

_____

_____

_____

_____

_____

_____

_____

_____

Factors which may fluctuate, change, etc.:

_____

_____

_____

_____

_____

_____

_____

_____

_____

Possible variations which may apply:

_____*Fill in the blanks*   _____*Generalizing with other stories*

_____*Checklist story*   _____*Story to address fears*

_____*Curriculum story*   _____*Judgment story*

*Ideas*_____

_____

_____

_____

Social Story Report

Name_____ Date_____/_____/_____

Story Title:_____

Support Materials or Activities:_____

Current Review Schedule:_____

Do you feel the story is having a positive impact? _____

Child's Current Response(s) to the targeted situation_____

_____

_____

_____

_____

Child's reaction to the story_____

_____

_____

Any problems with the story? No_____   Yes_____ Explain_____

_____

_____

Suggestions for revisions, etc:_____

_____

_____

Please return report to: **by:**

thank you...

Appendix B: Generic Social Story

<u>Standing in Line</u>

Sometimes people stand in lines.

People stand in lines for different reasons. There are standing lines, walking lines, slow lines, and group lines.

Standing lines are for waiting. Sometimes standing lines of people wait for everyone to get in line. Sometimes standing lines wait for the right time to start moving.

Standing lines don't always just stand. Sometimes people get tired of standing, and they move - they might scratch their head or move around a little. Sometimes when they move they touch people around them.

Standing lines usually become walking lines. Everyone who was standing, starts walking. In a walking line, people follow the person in front of them. Walking lines are for safely moving people from one place to another. Walking lines are used to move students in schools.

Slow lines are lines that move once in a while. People in slow lines stand, then walk a few steps, and stand again. Sometimes, the lines of people in a grocery store are like this. Sometimes, the lines at McDonald's are like this.

Appendix C: The Social Story Quiz

Directions: The purpose of this "quiz" is to raise awareness as to how the guidelines can be applied when writing for students with autism to possibly increase the clarity of a social story. Based on the guidelines for writing social stories, select the phrasing below which you feel would be most easily understood by a student with autism. Keep in mind effective stories have been written which deviated from guidelines.

---

1. _____   a) This is Joanna.

   _____   b) This is a nice picture of Joanna.

   _____   c) Joanna was smiling when this picture was taken. Many people like pictures of smiling children.

---

2. _____   a) Sometimes children have math problems they can't figure out.

   _____   b) Math is hard to do.

   _____   c) Children like to learn math.

---

3. _____   a) Don't talk loud in the library.

   _____   b) When I need to talk in the library, I will talk quietly and whisper.

   _____   c) Don't talk in the library.

---

4. _____   a) We go outside for recess.

   _____   b) We usually go outside for recess.

   _____   c) Children have fun at recess.

Answers to Writing for Children with Autism Quiz: 1-c, 2-a, 3-b, 4-b, 5-a, 6-b, 7-b, 8-b, 9-c

5. _____   a) Miss White sometimes talks to all the children at the same time. She does that when she wants to tell each child the same thing.

      _____   b) The teacher teaches the class.

      _____   c) Miss White talks to the class.

---

6. _____   a) There's no reason to be afraid of air hand dryers.

      _____   b) Air hand dryers are for drying hands. They turn off in about one minute.

---

7. _____   a) The substitute teacher is in charge.

      _____   b) Miss Johnson writes lesson plans for the substitute teacher. The lesson plans tell the substitute what to do.

      _____   c) Substitute teachers know what to do.

---

8. _____   a) I will sing quietly.

      _____   b) When I sing I will make sure I can hear the person singing next to me.

      _____   c) It's embarrassing to sing louder than everyone else.

---

9. _____   a) I go to school.

      _____   b) I go to school on Mondays, Tuesdays, Wednesdays, Thursdays, and Fridays.

      _____   c) I go to school on Mondays, Tuesdays, Wednesdays, Thursdays, and Fridays. Sometimes, we don't have school on those days. Mom or Dad will let me know if I don't have school.
